THE DIVINE TAVERN

BY ALI ASHRAF

This drunkenness began in some other tavern.
—*RUMI*

Dedicated to all the people of the world and beyond.

Preface

It is said by Sufis that to break the heart of an innocent human being is a greater sin than breaking the walls of Qa'aba, but why so? Because in heart, the perfect illusion (i.e. this beautiful universe) resides and when this illusion is broken, one begins to see reality as it is, which might lead to intense heartache. One begins to realise that all reality seems is, in reality, nothing but an illusion and what really is reality cannot be said or expressed. One is not left with much choice but to be sorrowful.

Sufis says that the tears that are shed at this stage of the spiritual journey are holier than the water on which Jesus walked, the water that kissed his blessed feet. The reason being is that these tears grow wings and fly to reach the throne of God and touch it, but it cannot be witnessed and neither can it be seen except by those who have pure souls.

The journey of the soul, if it is destined to reach God, will always pass through the abandoned valley of sorrows and heartache. Without tears, it is impossible to reach God, and without heartache, it is impossible to fall in love with him.

Unfortunately, we live in an age where tears are shed but for the wrong causes, where sadness prevails but because of the wrong reasons. In such a world, this poetry collection is an attempt to bring back the true meaning of tears and despair, and to bring back the pure cause that is worth crying for.

Contents

Beauty   1

Love   11

Grief   40

Death   64

God   75

Self   77

Sufi   86

Beauty

the garden

the chirping birds
they're your friends,
the shining sun
is your lamp.

the stars at night
are for you to play
to master your paintbrush
to give them shapes.

the bowing tree
is your shade
the grass underneath
is your bed.

the playful butterflies
they giggle when you see
they are gifts for you
from faraway fairies.

don't be sad my child
don't dwell in gloom
this world is your garden
and you are in it a flower
yet to bloom.

cruel beauty

behold, the sun looks
brighter today
did it come out from
where my love stays?

the sweetest of sweets
the cruellest of cruel
come, have a look
how in her town beauty rules

causing a massacre
just by gaze
she burns all that which is
warm and cool

her eyes are sharper
than a sword
her glow is more than
sun and moon

and whenever she wears
a red dress
it causes in town
a sweet unrest
people mistake her

for red rose
she can't be defined in
poetry or prose

from her body comes
a strange fragrance
cruel is that fragrance
and those eyes
just like wine
pouring down from skies
even angels become drunk
seeing her sight
and to get her even
the wise men fight
all those who claim
they are the wisest of wise
her one glance turns them
into fools.

she is the sweetest of sweets
the cruellest of cruel
she is a mixture of honey
and hemlock
sweet yet sour
and deadly too.

she is the sweetest of sweets
and cruellest of cruel.

a wine called eyes

let that wine pouring from your eyes
let that wine be my poison.
let your arms, fragile and soft,
let those arms be my grave.
let me stay in my grave
let me stay forever, I pray.
let the resurrection come and pass
because I won't be resurrected on that day
for better than the heaven is this place,
better is this grave in which I stay.

sweet forgetfulness

those bewitching eyes
made me forget the earth and sky.

alas! her fruitful lips
made me forget what was and is.

my bewildered soul,
don't cry because she is gone

but cry for she's taken away
what she brought with herself.

strange oblivion I did witness
while my head on her breasts.

I slept and wept, smiled and laughed
upon her comforting lap.

a new universe was created for me
within her tranquillizing embrace.

a transcending sweet forgetfulness
that was the state in which I stayed.

my shrine

you light up my world with just one glance
what will then happen if you'll advance to
dance?
my body will shiver, my world will tremble
drunkenness will overcome, my feet will
stumble.

your eyes make me drunk
your lips are cherry sweet
your arms are carved perfectly
by the master of masonry.

your hair, O those long curly hair
resting on your shoulders like they just don't
care
on every single curl clings my heartbeat
my heart skips a beat when you are here
my shrine will be made at your beautiful feet
infinite and eternal, I will always stay there.

eternal touch

touch me and make me eternal
one last touch is all I want
the sight of you I can't forget
love of you is all I want.

crying in the middle of night
falling deep in the deepest misery
shine again, O my love!
come to me with that glowing face
alas! the time of my last breath has come
come my love before death comes.

Love

always love

there's not enough hatred
to make me hate.
there's not enough failure
to disappoint me.

there's not enough madness
to make me mad.
there's not enough reason
in reasoning.

there's not enough goodness
to prevail.
there's not enough evil
to tempt me.

there's not enough happiness
to make me laugh.
there's not enough sadness
to sadden me.

but in love's case
I will always choose to love
never hate
even if love is left
of an atom's weight.

my love, my lady

when the cool winter breeze
will come to please.
I'll put my breath at your feet
my love, my lady.

when the shore will rise and roar
for you, I'll read
romantic poems of Keats
my love, my lady.

I'll make garlands for you
from rare breeds of faraway beads
and crown you with it
my love, my lady.

I'll always make you laugh
even when winter will pass
I'll be the warmth of your heart
my love, my lady

I'll create honey too from your words
for I've never heard
anything so sweet
my love, my lady.

I'll never let those pearls
fall over your cheeks
I'll always make you happy
my love, my lady.

nuptial night

when the Lord will shower his blessings
when in the time of spring
when flowers will bloom, birds will sing
when we'll exchange our rings
that, my love, will be the beginning.

then the day will pass alright
we'll be called man and wife
then will come the awaited night
I'll start by touching your thighs
the passion will rise like a tide.

your eyes, your hands so cold.
your body warm yet wet
my blood will move so quick
my body covered in sweat
everything we will forget

my arms on your back
your face on my neck
I will feel your breath
and your body will melt
within my arms dwell.

you'll bewitch me by the gaze
my hands wandering on you
treating you like a maze
and when I'll embrace
our blood will pace.

heavy panting will overcome
unconscious we'll become
sweetly pained your slender body
will be radiant like the sun
and your eyes pouring rum.

I'll take you by surprise
I'll kiss you upon your eyes
time will demise
universe will rejoice
beginning of joys

and all that will be done
to you my sweet maiden
that you've always craved
in your wildest imaginations.

two broken stars

two broken stars drifted apart
in sorrow, they almost died
then they decided to be one
then they shone, ah so bright!
the entire universe illuminated
because of their light

you know darling, who are those stars?
O, my love! me and you are.

let's wait for december to come

"let's wait for december to come"
in my ear, she whispered and sung
and her voice started to tremble
while thinking of coming November
when we would not be able to meet
but then she thought of december
on her face came a smile so sweet
the whole month of november
was between our next meeting.

in thinking all my time was vested
my patience was thoroughly tested
by november's each day
it felt so dry as hay
and in the longing I did stay
but what she said I did remember
and those words made numb
"let's wait for december to come"

sometimes it brought some mirth
that our next meeting would feel like rebirth
the nightingale sang and I heard
from far away came the chirping of birds,
songs of sorrow and some happy too

some told in longing, some in rejoice
and I wasn't left with much choice
but to remember her promise and yearn
and wait for december to come.

"at the corner of the street"
she said "we would meet
where the road turns
under the tree
whose branches hang lowly
and though winter would have come
but still, it'll all seem beautiful
to us lovers' eyes but till then my love
let's wait for December to come".

snow started falling so soon
full and brighter seemed the moon
I thought of morrow and couldn't sleep
then came our awaited noon
I sat under the tree to wait
hours passed and no one came
days past and I waited daily
the consequence was always the same.

I tried her number, it was off
I missed her face pale and soft

then came a letter at my address
that said she had found someone else,
that said she is forever gone
and I spent december all alone.

just a dream

whenever I see you in dreams
I try to make it last forever
but when I wake up after that
I try so hard to go back to sleep
just to dream you a bit longer.

we run in streets barefoot
not even caring what people think
careless and wanton we seem
when I kiss your tulip lips
not caring what people think.

our eyes sparkle when we meet
and those who don't even know us
know this that although crazy we seem
we really are crazy about each other
just by looking at the shine in our eyes
they begin to know these things.

oh, how much they envy us and our love
and when we laugh together
in our childish manners,
so much that it aches our stomach

they think it's inappropriate
but we know they are just jealous.

when I run my fingers through your hair
it makes you feel as if ecstatic is the air
and I touch you with my hands so tender
it makes you weak in your knees
and then I embrace your body so slender
and your entire body melts around me.

neither man nor God,
neither heaven nor hell,
I cannot comprehend what it is
that feeling is just a perfect bliss
but then I realise that
it's nothing but a dream
and just a dream it is.

dream victim

there was a time
whenever I dreamt of you
on that whole day
I had a smile on my face

but now my love
whenever of you I dream
it is a nightmare
it's so haunting.

I see your face
in every face
and your memory comes back
to taunt me.

why our paths crossed
and why they strayed away?
why this joke
on me fate played?

I have rocks
on my chest
I am a victim
of love's quest.

I feel alone
in crowds of thousands
and when I am alone
I weep soundless.

lonely stars, lonely me

lonely stars amidst midnight
when I look unto thee
reflecting on my tears
while twinkling you say to me
"O lonely soul, your world
it is filled with crowds of men
then why you look unto us
to spare your loneliness?"
while twinkling say to me
lonely stars amidst midnight
when I look unto thee.

remembering you

there you are
living the dream
here I am
with broken dreams
there you are
on a path of joy
and here I am
in grave misery.

here I miss you
all night long
there you stay
not missing me
the moon asks me
where your love has gone?
the stars keep on
teasing me.

in your life
you've seen success
failures have been my fate
since you've left
and in this longing
I live and dwell

my heart is broken
and all the pieces fell
into a well
filled with sorrows from hell

but when your image comes
in my mind
and news of you leading
a wonderful life
then in your happiness
my heart rejoices
and on my face
comes a smile
and everything seems
beautiful for a while.

vicious cycle

I am thinking of forgetting you
but in doing so I am remembering you
where should a man with a broken heart go?
what should a man with a broken heart do?

where lies the peace for my heart?
when will end this restlessness?
how should I get a fresh start?
when will end this cruel test?

tell me how should I forget you?
I remember you in the process of doing so
alas! this vicious cycle, this torment,
there is no escape. no place to go.

memories are puzzle, they are a maze.
look at the scars on my face
you were my only chance for grace
woe to my fate, I lost it with pace.

return!

return! my love, come
I don't have enough time left
this longing has made me weary
and I am going mad.

return! for I have no longer
any patience left
return! for since you have left
I am bereft.

return! just a glimpse of you
will be enough for me
return! so life can run in my veins
return! I want to live again

return! for I am no more
what I used to be
what will be the use of returning
when I won't be me?

I am sorry

I am sorry for falling in love with you
I am sorry for loving you like there's no
tomorrow

I am sorry for your smile meant the world to me
I am sorry that you are the source of my misery

I am sorry for believing in all you said
I am sorry for the tears that I have shed

I am sorry for being lost in your eyes
I am sorry for they were the source of my life

I am sorry for thinking you were my everything
I am sorry for committing this beautiful sin

I am sorry that at last, you have left me
I am sorry for thinking you were my destiny

I am sorry for all the memories of past
I am sorry that good times went so fast

I am sorry that I tried and gave my best
I am sorry without you I can find no rest

you don't be sorry, you shouldn't be
the only person who should be sorry is me.

I am burning

I put my heart at your feet
and you stomped all over it
you had me under your spell
O, you cruel flesh-eating witch.

you burned my soul by ignorance
you pierced skewers through my chest
you poured on it an evil essence
and cooked my flesh to the best.

you brought to the table my cooked heart
mingled in spices and sour sauce
you like an animal tore it apart
and ate it while making it art

but even after that and my body tore
I want you to hurt me more
I am addicted to your cruel nature
that's the thing I love you for.

a dialogue between heart and mind

heart:

If a mistake it is let's not resist
let's not think too much about this
let's make this beautiful mistake
and let this glorious love persist.

If it's a sin or a vulgar act
and one of the notorious things
let's commit this sin, be notorious
and see what pleasures this sin brings.

mind:

stay away from love
if you want to prosper
be logical, be reasonable
like a good philosopher.

love causes madness
and makes you lose your wits
a slow death it brings

a murder it commits.

heart:

what good is this philosophy
based on nothing but doubt?
It's been present for centuries
yet no answers it found

and death is the most inevitable thing
that we can't deny
let love become cause of our death
so, with pride, we must die.

mind:

don't get involved too much in love
it's not a sane thing to do
It brings pain and suffering
and brings affliction too.

it never brings a happy end
learn from lovers of the past
the world still cries at their fate
and those wailings forever last.

heart:

is it sane to be confused all the time
by questions on which reason insists?
questions so old yet unanswered;
does God exist? does man exist?

whereas love is blind in faith
no confusion it contains
and all lovers reach eternity
from those afflictions and pain.

mind:

don't let love break you, O heart,
don't be that much blind
for you are impossible to mend
you are one of a kind.

the heart is such a delicate thing
one must be careful with it
just like a glass, it gets broken
almost by the slightest of hits.

heart:

O glass, shatter into thousand pieces
for I've been so careful of you
taking care of you, night and day
only brought worry to be true.

O glass, break you miserable thing
break and let go of worry
I've been so careful all my life
now it's time for me to be free.

why can't I move on?

I want to forget how she looked like
I want to forget the way she smiled
but somehow in the happiest moments
when I am in a gathering of friends
her memory trespasses my laid boundaries
and her laughter echoes over my misery
what has she done to me?
why my heart feels so heavy?
why my heart is her throne?
why can't I move on?

from love to hate

everything's gone but the longing stays
It has been here for many days
It stays here to cheer me
and to keep me accompany
It tells me about you, my love,
and how I will meet you in the future
as many years will go by
or maybe in your arms I'll cry.

I will look for that look in your eyes
like the moon amidst the desert sky
in hot summer, on the desert night
reflecting on sand still shining bright
then look for your heart; is it cruel?
still, like the old days when you were here?
like the winter breeze so chilling and cool
unmoved like frost on mountains high.

are your arms still soft as snow?
with the pale and breathtaking glow?
or has age turned your outer self
as was your inner self:
cold-hearted, dry and cruel

and sometimes soft too.
O, my love! yes, I do miss
how carelessly I used to love you.

but you found happiness in your life
and I was blessed with grave longing
sometimes it makes it tough to survive
other times it makes me think
the way this world goes around.
how time changes everything,
how people leave others behind,
how people let others sink.

many years later I'll pass your door
and look at you with nothing more
but thought about this longing time
how I longed for you on lonely nights
and how by the time it demised
into empty space of nihilism
and think how I loved you the most
and now you are the one
I most despise.

Grief

reflections

brave is not the one
who is not afraid
but brave is the one
who in fear
overcomes it.

courage is not to do
some brave act
but it is to do
the right thing
regardless of
what people think.

lonely is not the one
who has no friends
but lonely is the one
who amidst friends
thinks of someone else.

sad is not the one
who cries a lot
but it is the one
who stays silent.

it's an art

to walk with a heavy heart
it's an art.
to begin again with a fresh start
it's an art.
to forget one's wretched past
it's an art.
to be constantly pricked by misery's dart
it's an art.
to be lovers and live apart
it's an art.

I've learned one thing
from the life I've spent
and chances I've missed
I am not an artist.

tormented soul

can you listen
to the chirping of morning birds?
they are singing songs for you
and do you know this
I waited with them
all night long for you?

in the meantime
I've made a new friend
my new friend is called
the moon
it waits for the sun
to show up
just as I
wait for you.

moon's desire
extinguishes at sunrise
but my beloved
can nowhere be found
I've waited for you
many a night
believing your words

"I'll come around"

when the sun comes up
and a new day starts
rejoice in happiness
moon and stars
awaited sun
finally comes for them all
and I cry alone
with my tormented soul.

kill me

your tortures have burned
my heart so much
now what's left
are ashes
come, my love,
and burn at once
what's left in my body
with matches.

you don't know
how much it hurts
your cruelty hurts more
than lashes
and now my heart
feels the same
as when on glass
rock smashes.

I am tired of living
in this state
half-alive
and half-dead
spare me from
this misery now

kill me so I can
move ahead.

new year

nothing new
about new year
still, they haven't called
whom I hold dear
still, from my eyes
fall these raining tears
still, torments of longing
my poor heart bears.

still, streets are filled with joy
but my heart is empty
still, people celebrate
and I am in misery
still, I stay alone
within my dreadful home
still, waiting for you to come
my sweet remedy.

world goes around
and times change
alas! my broken heart
it stays the same.

my story

how many tears I have cried?
I have lost the count
but I know that the river nile
is less watery than my eyes.

the clouds have borrowed rain from me
they all cry in my misery
I am the lord of sorrows and pain
it's my sighs that cause clouds to rain.

forever I will dwell in despair
no one to love, no one to care
no one to have my misery shared
no place where
I can get this heart repaired.

look you! carefully see
the angels are crying
the earth is shaking
the sky is dying
someone must have told them
my story

that is why the entire universe
is in mourning.

songs of sorrow

why do you want to kill me
with a sword in your hand?
I, who can die
by your bare glance.

O keeper of my heart!
O knower of my secrets!
I count hours and days
just to meet you again

you, who is my heaven
you, what's within it
you are the reason
I believe in it.

you are the reason
I am alive
you are the reason
I want to die
you are my sun
you are my moon
you are my sunrise

and my midnight.

only with you
I want to live
only with you
I want to converse
you are my everything
from beginning to the end
you are my world
you are my universe.

sad memories of past
no hope for tomorrow
without you what's left
are songs of sorrow.

purposelessness

high rise building
on the top floor lies
my luxury apartment
and when I look below
I see crowds crawling
doing their daily routines
achieving nothing in the end
taking nothing to their graves
It's all a purposeless race.

what is it that people do?

what is it that people do
that makes their eyes shine
when their lips move
and expand upwards?

I've seen lovers do it
those who are together
and I've seen others too
they call it "laughter"

I don't know what that is
maybe in childhood I did?
but now I don't remember
how should I do it?
and whenever I try to do
it just feels like déjà vu
cause I've forgotten all of it.

only sighs

no shoulder to rest my head upon
no lover to tap me on my back and say
"don't cry"

no one to take my hand and lead
"I am here for you," no one says
"just smile"

empty streets and grey skies
silver moon that shines at night
and only sighs.

there's no one outside

there's a noise outside
maybe a knock on my door
when I go out to see
it's just hustling of the shore

or maybe whispering of leaves
conspiring against me
to keep me inside
and to make me realise
that I am all alone.

a million hands every night
are raised to God in prayer
most of them rejected
just a few fulfilled
but then there's hope
and only hope it is
never bringing anything.

I stand up and go to the door
with the hope that you are here
but I can only look at the sea
bursting with energy
fighting against the shore

so intense and so deep
as if it's trying to say
"there's no one outside
it's only you and me"

absolute loneliness

my pain forces me to write
yet I try to disguise
my falling tears
behind happy eyes

but I can't fool myself
neither the person next to me
my eyes tell my story
they show my misery

they show that no one is here
no one to embrace me
or take me into arms
to spare my misery.

no one hears my cry
no one knows how lonely I am
no one knows my heart is bursting
with tears and only I have
to bear, no one to bear with me
in these harsh times
no one is here with me.

all my friends are long gone
I have no one left to share
the agony of my heart
even God doesn't answer my prayers
and release me from this pain I adhere

the person next to me on the bus
asks me "why do you look so sad?"
I look at him with tears in my eyes
and I answer him with sighs
"I have no one left"

deep wound

a distant voice echoes
cutting through the fog
passes my room's window
and rests upon my ear.

it reminds me of something strange
strange yet known
like a friend who meets
after a long time gone.

It makes me realise
that it is the voice of silence
that it is the voice of loneliness
that it is the voice of longing

and it reminds me
that in this vast world
not a single soul cares for me
that I am all alone

then I embrace my loneliness
and go to sleep
with tears in my eyes

and smile on my face
trying to hide from loneliness
that I am hurt deep.

shattered pieces of heart

shattered! shattered! shattered!
pieces! pieces! pieces!
my already broken heart
shattered further into pieces.

only thorns I do pick
no roses, no daisies
this loneliness aches my heart
your memory still teases.

more suffering after suffering
more pain after pain
happiness disappears
as sadness increases.

O pain, my only friend,
you were here till the end
and I am in a strange state now
not happiness but pain pleases.

being a man

it's unbearable,
unbearable to be a man,
to suffer while we live
after every failed plan.

to walk with the heavy feeling
of unrequited love
without any healing
and wounds more than enough.

to be subject to criticism
to be subject to change
when criticism one can't bear
when change one doesn't crave.

I was a careless child
a child full of pride
never cared for anything
to nothing, I did abide

but then I grew up
and rose like a tide

woe to my fate
as a child, I should've died.

I started to be careful
craved love and craved care
always wanted appraisal
insult I couldn't bear

but then reality struck me
no love and care I found
only unrequited love
that made severe wounds.

"How to be a complete man?"
with excitement, she asks me
I say "a thousand lonely nights,
a million broken dreams"

Death

come, my love!

you have no idea
how much I've longed
to kiss your lips

and to feel the embrace
of your bony arms
uncomfortable yet relieving.

how much I've missed
your eyes, your dark black-hole eyes.
come death! come, my love!
and take me by surprise.

broken

where's the market
where hearts are mended?
where do live
the healers of broken souls?

O God, end my misery
or else end me
in this world
I find no peace at all.

I have been wounded too much
and I cry tears of blood
when will come the glad tidings?
when will I be dying?

when shall my body become dirt?
and leave this wretched world?
I am tired of living, I have lost all hope
carrying these wounds for so long.

Oh tears, so many tears
how will I pass these coming years?

so much pain at an age so young
O death come, for I am done.

hell

they ask me to write humorous poems
but I don't know humour myself
just as I don't like to believe in heaven
but I do believe in hell
and I don't think there's eternal bliss
for I have never witnessed it
but about eternal damnation: yes,
I carry that within my chest.

roses and thorns

I went for the roses
got hurt by thorns
I think of times
been past, long gone
and here I stay alone
accompanied by misery
my heart is torn
for me my grave awaits
but I am already gone.
my friend, don't you know this?
life itself is a grave
and the burial was done
when I was born
and here I stay alone.

the end

It's neither near nor far
where you are
wandering in the universe
from an unknown hour
I couldn't reach there
for you are so high
and I dwell here
still learning to fly.

who am I?
nothing but a cry,
a lonely existence
on the seventh sky.
trust me when I say
that I try
kill me or hang high
and then crucify
for I am a lover
of a secret beloved
and like a true lover
I wish to die.

eternal ocean of love

dive into
the ocean of love
it doesn't matter
if you can't swim

the purpose is
not to be ashore
but it is
to die within.

the tyranny of life
must end
come death,
my awaited friend,

don't be afraid
it's not the end
let the joyous
eternity begin.

into deep
waters of love

let me die
let me sink.

I am no poet
nor a poetic soul
the world won't care
for losing me

yet I write
from my heart's blood
my woes and sighs
are my ink

lethal reconciliation

you took my day's comfort
you took my night's sleep
but you never gave in
yourself to me
and on lonely nights
I wander the streets
longing for the day
when our hearts will meet
and our soul will be one
when we'll dive deep
into the ocean of love
but now what's left
in my wretched life
are mourning and sighs
prayers and cries
I feel like I am a victim
of some disease
and this disease is love, I believe
and its cure will be found
when you'll embrace my body
with your arms around

then our souls will flee
and reach divinity.

God

I

I am in my own ecstasy
I don't need any other
I neither beget nor am I begotten
I have no father, no mother

Self

phoenix

landed on my shoulder
the awaited phoenix
from centuries it was wandering.
it was thought as
the granter of the kingdoms
broke many brave hearts
left many wondering

what all the ambitious
and brave men sought
not even a glimpse
never appeared to them.
they say in its search
great Alexander fought
with its lucky touch
he could've ruled
seas and continents.

in the heavens
and on the earth
from centuries
it wandered free

soaring high
in vast skies
to grant its kingdom to be
no matter
how much it flew
no matter
wherever it'd be
that glittery
shiny bird
never saw
someone worthy.

Its wings are glittery
green from outside
from the inside
in orange, they shine
Its body shines
like sunlight
turning the seeker
almost blind.

some nights ago
I saw it in my dream
landing on my shoulder
smoothly

first its touch
scared me
I thought "what does this bird
want from me?"

I didn't know
what it meant
I was shocked to witness
that event
maybe it was a sign
for the times
that are nearing
landed on my shoulder
the awaited phoenix
from centuries it was wandering.

who am I?

"who am I?" my heart cries
finds no answer as time flies
burned by love it becomes a flame
puts the burning fire to shame.

vanished self
searches for its own self
a divine intervention it craves
wants to get rid of all desires
finds nothing but burning fire.

"who am I?" my heart cries
to itself my heart replies
"trapped inside a beloved's body
a lover's soul made to fly"

"who am I?" my heart cries
"all that is, is nothing but I"

be

be my heaven
be my hell
be my thirst
be my well

be my sky
be my land
be my water
be my sand

be my sun
be my moon
be my melody
be my tune

be my meeting
be yearning
be my destiny
be journey

be my atom
be my soul

be my nothing
be my all

be where I'd go
be where I'd be
be you, be me
be my everything

I am

I can burn you whenever I want
and whenever I want
I can extinguish
I am both
your thirst and your well
and I know you want
all of it.

sun has borrowed
its fire from me
I burn within
my own fire
I am the cause
of my flame
I am my own desire.

before the beginning
there was I
after the end
I will be
I am the reason
I stay alive

I am the reason
I die.

Sufi

the cup of jamshed [1]

not in the future
not in the past
everything is temporary
nothing can last
each moment is cut
by the time's sword
everything is bound
to a specific hour.

it's a bitter truth
that I can't escape
my end is also written
on destiny's page
that time is near
when someone will call,
from the other side
someone will call my name.

it brings tears to my eyes
yet it amazes me;

---

[1] Cup of Jamshed is a cup in Persian mythology and literature known to have the elixir of immortality in it.

the nothingness in everything
nature's tyranny.
when every start is already pregnant
with its end
then why, oh my poor heart,
you dream of infinity?

oh you, the blessed one,
fetch me a wine;
a wine so pure
a wine so divine
a wine whose drunkenness
will forever be
from now till the end
from there to eternity.

request to master rumi[2]

as high as the skies with no limits
as deep as the depths of the arabian sea.

his knowledge wanders in the universe
wanders for a broken heart to heal.

O master Rumi, you are the healer of sick
and mine is the heart that craves to be healed.

be the healer to this crying heart
as Shams cured yours, with love it was filled.

like you became a healer to the poet of the east[3]
when he wandered at nights in streets.

added the honey of love to life
his sore verses, you turned them sweet.

awake! master Rumi, someone is calling you.
awake! from your shrine's peaceful sleep.

---

[2] Rumi was a famous Persian poet and a Sufi saint
[3] Poet of the east is the honourable title given to Muslim poet Allama Muhammad Iqbal, who is said to be the spiritual disciple of Rumi.

now another nightingale[4] cries for rose.
now another heart needs to be healed.

---

[4] nightingale is a metaphor for "poet" in Persian literature

dialogue between a dervish [5] *and impatient youth*

dervish:

do not hate 'hatred'
for hatred is all we have
losing this divine gift
we will become beggars with no means.
no means to continue this act called life
we won't be able to continue this scene.

young boy:

but dervish isn't hatred an enemy of love?
love that is divine and high up above
love that makes honey sweet
without love all is nothing but a dream.
love brings all illusions to life
and from mere thoughts creates reality.

---

[5] dervish is another name for wandering Sufi saints

dervish:

you talk well, O child of mine,
but you don't know the plan of divine
this world is a stage of yours and mine
for which nature created opposites,
opposites to make
this divine poem rhyme.

silence

"is it the worldly matters?
is it caused by the heavens?
why are you acting so strange?
what is the cause of those sealed lips?

have you lost a lover?
are you going insane?
are you wanting money?
or are you in pain?

you used to speak a lot
you were a joyous man
what has happened to you?
is it something that I did?

why don't you speak a single word?
why no expressions on your face?
tell me are you deeply hurt?
or is it just a phase?

is this because of
what's happening in the world?
all those wars and violence?"

I reply "No, my friend
truth begets silence."

lost

the fragrance
of your curls
intoxicates me
like a dervish
I spin and whirl
lost in your trance.

Oh, my beloved,
I am lost, so lost
in my soul
in your soul.
where am I going?
where did I come from?
I don't know
what path I am on.

ecstatic dance

let's sing
let's dance
let's create romance.
in love
let's fall
us all.

let's bear
the spear
of beauty's glance.
on the lover's path
take a stroll
us all.

O world!
hold my hand
take this chance.
let's respond
to love's call
us all.

why be sober?
why not

drunk and intense?
this love's wine
is here for
us all.

lose senses
get lost
in love's trance.
being sober
is not good
at all.

the divine tavern

by Allah[6]
by the night when Muhammad[7] the prophet
to heavens ascended.

by heavens
that are in numbers seven
by this divine tavern[8].

by the glimpse of beloved's face
by the time that passes with pace
by love's eternal grace.

by the lock of Jesus's[9] hair
by a dervish without care
by beloved's face so fair.

---

[6] God in Islam, often called "beloved" or "friend" by Sufis
[7] Muhammad (S.A.W.W), founder of Islam, who is believed to be last and the final messenger by Muslims. He is also revered by Sufis as the perfect being and source of all illumination.
[8] The entire creation, the cosmos, the universe, is symbolized as a tavern in Sufism and all the things living in it are unknowingly drunk in the ecstasy of cupbearer i.e. God
[9] lock of Jesus's hair is said to be the source of immense power and miracles, some cults believe it to hold such powers that if used in sorcery, one could enthral souls of all humanity.

by love's divine wine
by all that is yours
by all that is mine.
I am drunk!

Please leave your reviews on Amazon.

Follow Instagram for more poetry and updates:
aliashraf_poetry

Milton Keynes UK
Ingram Content Group UK Ltd.
UKHW021037170924
448459UK00014B/673